I Give You My Word

A Journey to the Self
Through Words and Watercolor

free
ME. *fre*
OE. *freo,*
G. *frei* < IE. ba
Sans. *priyá-,* dea

noble, glad,
illustrious

8. not literal; not exact
[a *free* translati

1. *a)* not under contr
some arbitrary powe

not in
bonda

not
opposed

having
liberty

open
[a *free*
road
ahead]

Crow 95

I Give You My Word

A Journey to the Self
Through Words and Watercolor

Written and Illustrated
by
Janice Crow

Starwae Press
Sonoma, California

Photography by Janice Crow & John Curry
Designed by John Curry
Printed in Singapore

Publisher's Cataloging in Publication
(Provided by Quality Books, Inc)

Crow, Janice
    I give you my word : a journey to the self through
words and watercolor / written and illustrated by Janice Crow
    p. cm.
    ISBN 0-9753700-0-6

    !. Crow, Janice--Family. 2. Crow, Janice--Childhood
    and youth. 3. Painters--United States--Family relationships.
    4. Self-culture.   I. Title.

ND237.C8426A3 2004   759.13
                QBI33-2067
Library of congress Control Number: 2004091415

I Give You My Word may be ordered directly from:
Starwae Press
Sonoma, California
starwae.com
starwae@vom.com
800 793-4792

Lovingly dedicated to the Adams sisters
My mother Pearley, and Aunts Bennie, Nina, Eudie, Ivy and Vila

He was still too young to know that the heart's memory eliminates the bad and magnifies the good, and that thanks to this artifice we manage to endure the burden of the past.

Gabriel Garcia Marquez

contents

Foreword

From an early age I loved words and art. But my home had no books and certainly no concept of art. Everything I wanted to be and do was somewhere else.

My parents had eighth grade educations, four children my father didn't want, a terrible relationship. Pulling myself up by the bootstraps meant first I needed to earn money to buy the boots. This is the story of how I became an artist, charting the route as I went, mapping my way to self discovery.

As an adult, I had blocked out many memories of my own childhood, the good memories as well as the bad. In the course of doing this series of paintings, poems, and stories, I recovered many of those memories. Discovering and freeing the confident, creative, healthy child through this work, I've come to trust her playfulness, humor, tenacity and wisdom.

It all began one winter day as I was cleaning my studio. I took out a large box of family pictures, thinking once again that I should organize them into albums. Another box was full of clippings, quotes, cartoons, and inspiring articles that I'd saved ever since I could remember. There were "Peanuts" cartoons from the sixties, still as relevant and funny as ever.

I started sorting and organizing that day. It was cold and raining outside. I built a fire and began looking through the boxes. Hours passed like minutes as I became engrossed in the images and memories. The project grew into several weeks. Each day I looked forward to the time I could devote to it, putting off other things I needed to do whenever possible. I put the pictures, quotes, and cartoons in an album, arranging them in ways that seemed to fit, to tell a story. The story was my own life.

About a year later, I began the watercolors based on those childhood snapshots. The more I painted, the more I remembered about my life. Many days I would be working with tears in my eyes. Other days I'd be laughing.

That's when I started to write. As I wrote, still more memories surfaced. Through the experience, I've reclaimed my childhood in ways which have healed the past.

Words saved my life. Art gave me vision. History gave me perspective.

As I work these images talk to me
        tell me stories
                    reassure me
                            remind me that
I am always beginning

This is an experiment
                in the beginning
I'm exploring memory
                layers of meaning
        obscurity
                clarity

How time and focus and experience
        changes how we remember
                what has happened to us
        where we've been
                and how we remember this

How meanings of words and meaning
        of experience changes over time

This work brings out the part of me
        that is willing to
                take a risk
                        explore
                find origins
                        be original
                follow my heart
                        find out what's next

Begins again
                forgets to be afraid
        is spontaneous
                        celebrates
Is valid
        authentic
                enthusiastic
                        beginning

light¹ (līt)

L. *lumen*,
lucere, to shine

1. *b)* a form
of radiant energy

in·teg·ri·ty *n.*
see INTEGER]

being complete; unbroken
2. the quality or state of
being unimpaired; perfect

Crow Is My Name

"Caw! Caw! Hey, Crowbait!" the boys yelled every day as they followed me home from school. Why couldn't my name be Smith or Jones? I was glad to change it to Lacey at age seventeen by marrying my childhood sweetheart.

Even after divorcing and marrying again a couple of more times, I kept the last husband's name rather than going back to Crow. My relationship with my father was painful as a child and distant as an adult. But when I became a painter and started exhibiting work, I wanted my own identity, even if it meant taking my father's name.

During this time I happened to read about crows in a bird book . The book described the crow's characteristics of sagacity, adaptability, and intelligence. The name Crow was much more appealing in that context. I had often incorporated words into my painting, and decided to combine a picture of a crow with the word "integrity."

Later, I was looking through some childhood pictures and thought of combining the word integrity with a drawing of myself at age two. As I drew, I moved into a state of reverie, realizing that the drawing was communicating to me. The meaning of integrity, "perfect, unbroken condition," was about my own essence, regardless of what had happened to me in my life. The perfection of the innocent child, the enthusiasm, the spirit, was still within me and needed expression.

In writing a letter one day, the word "important" came to mind. Selecting another snapshot, I began to draw, and realized that I bore a resemblance to my father in that picture. As I thought about him and drew, a feeling of well-being came over me. I was recreating my image of myself. All my life, because of the way my father treated me as a child, I had an underlying feeling of being worthless and unimportant. As I did this drawing, aware of the meaning of the word important, "to have much significance, value, influence, power, authority, high position," I felt myself begin to embody the definition. Now when those old feelings of worthlessness come up I know they're just empty ghosts.

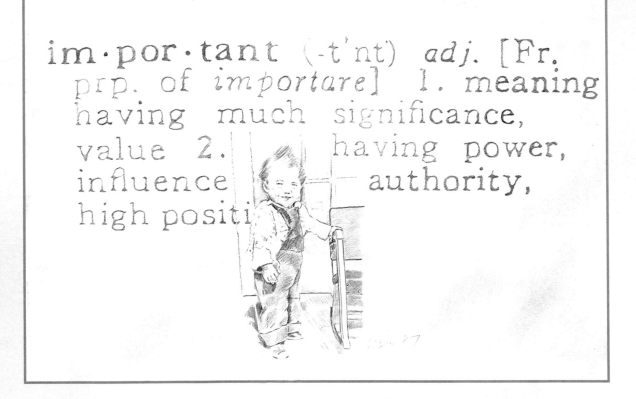

im·por·tant (-t'nt) *adj.* [Fr. prp. of *importare*] 1. meaning having much significance, value 2. having power, influence authority, high positi

Next came will, "the power of making a reasoned choice, energy, and enthusiasm." Many words followed. With each one, a deeper part of myself is realized. I now claim the characteristics of the bird that my name symbolizes. I am Janice Crow.

Family Trees

"What a good book the story of the Adams family would be," Aunt Bennie always said. By now our family includes members of just about every racial and sexual persuasion, and enough misfits and eccentrics to people a soap opera. As the only artist, I'm a misfit... my father asked me once, "Where did you come from?"

My mother and father met in the shipping department at Sears in 1935. Their families moved to Dallas from East Texas during the Depression, when farms had turned to dust. Family origins were sketchy at best. Probably the ancestors were sharecroppers in the South before coming to Texas.

Family pictures show poor East Texas farmers. The cabin my mother lived in was still standing when I was a girl, and we would go "down to the farm" for the day and take a picnic. The vacant farm was never sold because it wasn't worth anything. The cabin had two rooms with an open fireplace for cooking and heating. Grandmother did the wash in a big cast iron washtub outside. They drew water from a spring down the hill and brought it home in buckets. Bathing was in the creek all summer and a kitchen washtub in winter. The family crest could have read, "When it's too tough for the rest, it's just right for me."

Great grandmother Crow was full-blooded Cherokee. She had coal black hair when she died at age ninety four. The rest of my heritage was, my father used to say, "Heinz 57 Varieties," mostly Scotch-Irish and English. Both families were proud of their roots, at least the ones they knew about. When I asked where my mother's grandfather was from, they said "Well, we don't exactly know. He came riding in on a horse from the east." On my father's side they knew only that his father was not born in wedlock, and beyond that was a mystery.

When my mother was three years old her father died, leaving grandmother with ten children to raise alone. The oldest boy, Raymond, became the man of the house at fourteen. They survived by following the harvest across Texas, picking cotton, corn, beans, moving on to the next field until harvest was over. Aunt Bennie remembers as a child being under the wagon in the shade all day, watching the baby while the older children worked alongside their mother.

I think of my and my husband John's family as opposite ends of the orchard in a family tree comparison. His family, from Pennsylvania and with listings in the Blue Book, can trace their history back to before the Mayflower, to England and Germany. When the University of Pittsburgh published a biography of the Spencer branch of his family, I gave Aunt Bennie a copy. After reading "The Spencers of Amberson Avenue," recounting the trials of that family, she mused, "You'd think they'd have been happy. After all, they had shoes."

Pearley May Adams

My mother didn't like her name. She would say, "Don't call me Pearley May, call me Pearley Will!"

She was born in Reese, Cherokee County, in East Texas, the seventh of ten children born to my grandmother by the time she was thirty three. The children walked to the one room school three miles up the road. Lunch was usually biscuits left over from breakfast.

After the eighth grade, Pearley left school because it didn't seem to her that what she needed to know was coming from the classroom. She was ashamed of her hand me down clothes. With few choices in 1931, she lived with her married sister and tried to find work. Eventually she found a part-time job at Sears, and met my father there. They were married, but it was not true love on her part. It was a way to get away from her lecherous brother-in-law. My father seemed nice enough, and she thought love would follow.

It didn't. David Crow was extremely possessive and jealous, even of her family and us children. He wanted her to stay home and do nothing except wait on him. He didn't like the way she was naturally the life of the party. They came home from any social gathering in a fight. We were happiest when he was out of town on business.

In spite of her unhappy marriage, Pearley was a wonderful mother. She was a great comedienne, entertaining us children with her made up farm girl games, like making a chicken she had beheaded and plucked do naked dances on the counter top, working it like a puppet before cutting it up to fry for dinner. For dessert, she made fudge candy or caramel popcorn balls, and we would help her, "licking the bowl," and forming the sticky popcorn into balls. She taught me to cook, to make pies with crust made from scratch.

When I was a teenager my friends gathered around her at our parties to hear her latest jokes and stories. She learned our rock and roll dance steps and taught me the Charleston. A great acrobat, she spent endless evenings when my father was out of town attempting to teach me to walk on my hands, do cartwheels, and bend over backwards. I never got the hang of it.

Pearley

won·der (wun'dər) *n*. [ME < OE
1. a person, thing, or event that
causes astonishment and
admiration;

2. to have curiosity or doubt about;
want to know

know (nō)
1. a clear perception

be sure of
[to know that one
is loved]

Mother's Biscuits

My mouth waters remembering the smell of my Mother's biscuits, hot out of the oven. I liked watching her make them the old fashioned way, just like her mother had done it on the farm. She sifted flour into a large mixing bowl, then with her fingers curled into a soft fist, made a small crater in the center. She added a pinch of baking soda and some Crisco shortening, mixing it until it was the texture of tiny pebbles. Pouring in just enough buttermilk, she worked it slowly and rhythmically, rolling it into a ball. When just enough flour was absorbed to make perfect dough, she gently shaped it into round biscuits. They tasted like love.

The Pleasure Queen

"Hold this up to your ear and listen." Aunt Eudie handed me a sea shell, white, spiky and rough on the outside, smooth and pink inside. "Do you hear the ocean?" I did. It was magic, hearing "whoosh" in my ear. Even more wonderful, Eudie was talking to me, not baby talk most other people babbled. It was the first time I remember being addressed as a person. I loved her for that.

There were eight cousins. Our mothers, three sisters, were raising us without much help, except for our grandmother and Eudie, the fourth sister. Eudie wanted children of her own, but didn't have any. That was lucky for us, because we needed her.

I loved spending the night at Eudie's house. Classical music played on the radio... The Nutcracker Suite, Pines of Rome, Beethoven. The rooms were filled with roses from her garden. She followed her own rules... "It's OK to eat your dessert first, they do that in Holland." When she made these declarations, we never questioned her.

"Come on, get in the car, let's go," Eudie would say, throwing on one of her hats. Off we would go, to the zoo, the aquarium, Weber's Root Beer Stand. She always took us to the Texas State Fair in the fall. We called her the "Pleasure Queen." As she drove the eight of us around, sometimes she would get distracted and be stopped for some minor traffic violation, but between seeing all of us and hearing her 'I Love Lucy' sounding explanation, the policemen never did give her a ticket.

In her heart, Eudie was an artist, and inspired the artist in me. When we went to art museums, she always appreciated the most contemporary and avant garde work as well as the more traditional. Robert Rauschenberg was a favorite of hers. Although she had no education or art training, she had an innate understanding of good art, and encouraged me by saving early works of mine. I remember one painting from high school which at the time I thought didn't look "real" enough. Eudie saved it, and hung it in her living room. Years later I could see that in fact it was a delightful piece.

She made friends easily. Once when we went shopping, a very good looking young man waited on us in the shoe department. When he went to get the right size, Eudie whispered to me, "Janice, give him your card." After he came back, she struck up a conversation with him, found out he was from Switzerland, and didn't know too many people yet. By the time we left, thanks to her he had my phone number.

As a young woman, Eudie moved to Dallas from the family farm. She worked in an office building downtown. Looking out the window one day, she spotted a handsome man in an office across the street. Always adventurous and impulsive, she waved, smiled, caught his attention and wrote her telephone number in the air with her finger. He called, and not long after they were married.

de·light
infl. by LIGHT²]

1. to give great joy

Eudie's husband, J. C., died when she was 49. Without enough income to live on her own, she lived with various family members, a few months at a time. There was always competition about who would get to have her next. She was never meddling, and did not give advice unless asked, and usually not even then.

Once when I was very frustrated about a boyfriend's attitude and wanted Eudie's sympathy, she said simply, "There's a lot of different people in the world and a lot of different ideas..." without looking up from the apple pie she was making. Never judgmental, she was always ready to see all sides. When she heard I was getting a

divorce, her comment was, "Well, the one I feel sorry for is Spooky." He was our Chihuahua. Only once I remember she felt pressed to intervene. She prefaced her advice with, "Janice, fifty eight knows more than twenty eight." I knew I needed to listen.

In times of pure pleasure, I miss her the most... when I travel, or see an art exhibit I know she would love, and in Spring, when tulips and roses come into bloom.

My advice to you is not to inquire why or whither, but to just enjoy your ice cream while it's on your plate... that's my philosophy.
Thornton Wilder

Aunt Nina

"Nina, why do you put up with all these strays and misfits you're always taking in?" I asked Aunt Nina once, as yet another person 'down on his luck' was moving in temporarily to avail himself of her generous hospitality. (I had been a beneficiary of her "open door policy" more than once myself.) There was always room for one more at her dinner table...no advance notice necessary.

"Well, Janice," she replied, "like it says in the Good Book, we never know when we may be entertaining angels unaware."

ts of two colors, es

d horse or

pēs

pettis, al

art or frag

ection, di

f and dis

single t

a) an a

painting, drama,

of nonsense, busin

Wedding Picture 1943

This is a picture of Aunt Bennie's first wedding.
It was big and formal, the way they're s'posed to be.
But they forgot to bring flowers
for the flower girl...me.

The bride looks stiff, like she's posed.
The groom looks like a clown...he was.
My mother, a bridesmaid, looks happy,
she loved parties.

I look angry, disappointed,
the way the bride would feel, later.

Uncle Raymond's Farm

Uncle Raymond's garden has a grape arbor and a big fig tree. My cousin Raymond Arlen and I chase butterflies around the red and yellow zinnias. We eat bunches of purple grapes hanging from the arbor, then climb the fig tree to taste the fat juicy fruit hiding under its leaves. We swing together on swings that hang from the giant oak tree. At night we chase fireflies, and they sit on our hands with their lights flashing on, off, on, off.

swing

backw___d forward
freely

4. freedom to do as one wishes
(given full *swing* in the matter)

hon·or

1. high regard
2. a keen sense of right

Uncle Otis

This is Uncle Otis when he came through Dallas with the United States Army 112th Calvary on a troop train. Stopping for only twenty minutes, he couldn't get off. The whole family went down to see him and held me up to him. This picture was in the Dallas Morning News the next day.

The only time I ever saw my grandmother cry was the day they delivered the telegram about Uncle Otis. She cried and cried. The telegram said he was killed by "friendly fire." I was confused and angry. How can it be called "friendly fire?"

Is Everybody Happy? Yes, When 112th Pulls In

—News Staff Photos.

Hundreds of Dallas citizens besieged the Union Terminal for a glimpse of and a brief visit with the boys of the 112th Cavalry. But they weren't a bit more delighted (upper photo) to see the boys than were the boys to see them. The same goes for Corp. Carl Bond of Grand Prairie (lower left), Troop A, who indicated considerable interest at being met by Miss Doris Sanders of the same community. And who do you think was glad to see her uncle? None other than Janice Louise Crow (lower right) who was lifted to the train.

lessons from childhood

lessons from childhood

lessons from childhood

in·no·cent
1. pure

b) without guile or cunning; artless

The Contest

It's a sticky hot summer day. I'm four, going next door to play with Ronnie. His house is built on piers, high enough underneath to be a great playhouse. It's dark and smells old. The only light comes from a small opening where we go in. The soft damp dirt squishes between our toes. The cool air feels good on our sweaty skin.

We play with his trucks, make forts and roads, pretend we're pirates or cops and robbers. Squatting in our shorts, I notice Ronnie's penis, so different from me. He shows me how he pees, aiming it and making an arc. I'm amazed.

I have to find a way to pee like Ronnie. I run back to my house. My mother is doing laundry in the kitchen, with her wringer washing machine rolled up to the sink. I spot something I can use...a short drain hose sticking out the side of the washer.

"Mama, can I use that?"

"What for?"

"I need it."

"OK," she says.

I run back outside to show Ronnie. Now I can aim like he did.

"Let's have a contest to see who can pee the farthest!"

We stand on his front steps, high enough to give us some range. Ronnie goes first, arcing out over the grass a pretty good distance. Now it's my turn. Spreading my feet apart a little, like he did, I place the hose between my legs, pointing it slightly upward, just like he did.

Shocked, I feel the wet dribble down my leg, puddling on the step.

Ronnie, a true friend, doesn't laugh.

☆**bud·dy**

1. a close friend

2. partnership

The Battle

"I'm going to run away from home!" I stomped out of the kitchen, angry with my mother.

"OK Janice," Mother said. "Do you want me to help you? You'll need some food, so I'll make a sandwich for you."

NOT the response I expected. Now I had to follow through with my threat. I got as far as the front porch...then sat down to think about the situation. Too scared to go any further, I couldn't go back inside. I waited. "She would come looking for me pretty soon, and beg me to come back," I thought.

Time passed... No mother. The sandwich was long gone. I smelled dinner cooking. Finally, I could wait no longer. I had to give in, but how to do it and save face.

I thought about what they said in Sunday School, about the Devil always trying to win us over to his side, but if we asked Jesus for help, then the Devil could not win.

I found my mother in the kitchen. "Mama," I said, "I decided not to run away. Jesus and the Devil had a fight about it, and Jesus won."

ras·cal
[ME. rascaile
rogue;
scamp

Crow 95

The Bet

I couldn't wait to get home with the candy rocks I'd found on vacation at a souvenir shop. The candy looked real mixed in with rocks from the driveway.

"Betcha I can eat one," I said, showing my hand full of rocks.

"No you can't," said the neighborhood kids as they all pulled out their pennies for the bet.

Picking out the candy rock from the real ones, I chewed it up.

"How did you do that?"

"Easy," I said.

mis·chief

< OFr. < *meschever*

3. a tendency to vex with playful tricks
b) harmless spirits

Expression

"Get in step, Janice. Sing in key, Janice. Smile, Janice."

Her voice still echoes when I see this picture. I'm not the only one without a smile. Everyone in the class was nervous, waiting for the next criticism. The teacher never smiled.

Casting us in roles for a musical, she insisted that I take the role of a boy. She said because I had brown hair and was taller. The blond haired girls got the girl parts.

"I'm not a boy," I told her. My plea fell on deaf ears. I'd always loved performing until that class. For many years after her class I didn't sing except in the bathtub.

star

self-luminous
1. to perform
brilliantly

Color Lesson I

During World War II there was rationing of butter.
Instead we had white margarine which came with a
packet of orange gold powder to color it. Mother
taught me how to mix it. The orange marbled through
the white as I stirred... slowly blending until the whole
mixture was pure yellow.

stud·y

2. careful atten-
tion to, critical
examination of

Fall down seven times, get up eight.
Buddhist quote

te·na·cious (tə nā's
tenere, to hold:
3. that holds together
retains well;
strong

tough
5. persistent

Lesson II

I made a painting of a winter tree in my fourth grade art class. It was good.
But when I showed it to the teacher, he just said 'uh huh' in a bored way.
I was discouraged for a few years until I figured out that that teacher didn't
know a good tree from a hole in the ground.

Black and White

In Sunday School they taught us to sing,
    "Red and yellow black and white,
    we are precious in his sight.
    Jesus loves the little children of the world."

But I noticed that when black people came to our church, they were ushered to the balcony, and I saw a lot of people staring at them as if they didn't belong in our church at all. Sometimes I would even hear, "Why don't they go to their own church where they belong?"

It didn't make sense to me. What about the words, "Red and yellow black and white?"

I started to notice other things too, like when I counted all the begats in the Old Testament. It was clear to me that the world was a lot older than the generations numbered since Adam and Eve. Dinosaurs were older than a few thousand years.

Then I wondered why everyone seemed to blame Eve. Who wouldn't want to "eat from the tree of knowledge" to learn all they could? I was in fourth grade and I loved learning about things. And anyway, if Adam didn't want to eat the apple, all he had to do was say so.

reb·el (reb''l)
rebellare
resistance against
established
authority or
controls

The Explorer

Pushing his little wheelbarrow, Johnny was halfway down the long driveway leading to the road when his cousin Ann saw him.

"Johnny, where are you going?"

"I'm following my wheelbarrow," he said.

ex·plore

1. look into closely
examine carefully;

finding my way

The Flying Lesson

In the copilot seat with my hands on the dual controls, I feel the nose lift as the pilot pulls back on the wheel. Suddenly we're in the air, gaining altitude. On the rudder pedals, my feet move in rhythm as we bank into a turn. Looking out over the flat Texas countryside, I can see forever. I never want to come down.

It was 1955. I was 16. My boyfriend and I were out for a Sunday ride in his black '49 Ford coupe when I saw the billboard... RIDES $5.00 RED BIRD AIRPORT.

"Jack, let's do it."

I'd never been up in an airplane before. Jack was in a good mood that day.

"Okay," he said.

We pulled into the airport and paid the money. My heart raced as we climbed into the bright yellow Piper airplane. Taxiing down the runway, I was fascinated by the instrument panel; the heading indicator, the magnetic compass, the attitude indicator, with its tiny wings, showing whether the plane is flying up, down, or straight and level.

That day I decided to be a pilot. But how? Flying lessons were fifteen dollars an hour. My after school job at Walgreen's paid eighty five cents an hour. Weeks went by. I kept thinking, how can I do it? Finally, I had an idea. Maybe I could work at the airport in exchange for lessons.

"No," the manager said, "we only hire boys to wash and gas the planes, but I would give you free lessons if you would..." Can you imagine? The old creep thinking I would do that, with him?

I went back to my other priorities. Finish high school. Go to college. Marry the right man. Growing up in the fifties, these goals were equally important. The idea was, after you found the right man, you stood behind him, and helped him be what you wanted to be. There was even a song about it, "Stand By Your Man..."

Sky King

There had to be something more
than Biglow Street
The unpaved road
filled with dust and dogs
and children running around like strays
Where men came home dirty
and sometimes drunk
Women stayed home wondering
how they got stuck there
what happened to their dreams

Friday evenings
lying on the floor beside the Philco
I flew with Sky King
Going on his adventures
I resolved to be a pilot someday
Fly out of Texas
Solo

Diligent about my role, at age seventeen I married Jack, who seemed right at the time. I went to college at night, majoring in psychology and art. By the time I was 20, it was clear to me that I wasn't stupid, even though Jack kept trying to convince me I was. My job paid as much as his, and my college grades were better. I left.

I got a job with Braniff Airlines. Women were not hired as commercial pilots in those days, so that possibility was out of my reach, but at least with passes I could fly anywhere. I met men who took me up in their private planes... "Janice, let's fly up to Tanglewood and have lunch."

" Janice, I'll be in New York this weekend, can you meet me?" It was all very glamorous to this young girl from the wrong side of the Trinity River.

It was fun, but I soon learned it's not where you go, it's who you're with. During this time I'd met Charlie out by the pool at the apartment where I lived. He wasn't rich and didn't own a plane, but I'd be at Trader Vic's having Mai Tais and lobster tail with 'What's his name,' wishing I was with Charlie in his yellow '53 Chevy convertible, having hamburgers at the Rancho Drive In.

Well, through just plain dogged determination on my part, and the fact that one by one his roommates were all getting married, Charlie married me. Only trouble was, after a few years, I could tell his heart wasn't in it. I took my broken heart and moved on. Quitting the airline, I left for Europe and traveled for a few months.

That's when I started the list of qualities of the perfect man for me. Love hadn't worked, so I tried reason. Still going to college at night, I met Dennis in the college cafeteria. Dennis, my logic said, was a good choice. He was sweet, kind, dependable, getting his masters degree in accounting. Dennis and my logic got married. My heart asked, "What are you doing?"

The following year, Dennis and I moved to San Francisco. One day, as I was going across the Golden Gate Bridge on my way to work, I heard a voice deep inside. " Janice," it said, "wake up." Dennis and I divorced. I went back to Dallas to regroup. Aunt Nina always had a place to stay for those "in transition."

o·rig·i·nal

1. having to do
with an origin;
initial; first;
earliest

never
occurred
or
existed
before

capable of thinking or acting
in an independent, individual,
fresh way

The airlines weren't hiring. I waited tables at Denny's while I figured out what to do. There I was, 32 years old, and so far, by traditional accounting, I was in the hole. Three failed marriages, two good jobs given up, no security, still a college student.

What was I doing? Where was I going? What was the line in that song? "Freedom's just another word for nothing left to lose..." Well, I was free. I could start over. From the beginning.

I still wanted to fly. I would go take lessons. Start. No need to have a man to buy the plane. It cost $22.00 an hour. The rest of my Denny's paycheck went to Aunt Nina for room and board. How simple. All those years, all that time, I could have been a pilot.

In my first lesson I learned how the sleek little Cessna naturally wants to fly. As weeks went by I learned to do takeoffs and landings, practicing the touch and go again and again. I learned to come out of a stall, to maneuver out of a spin.

On the day of my first solo, I'm calm, energized, ready. This is the day I've waited for since I was sixteen, back at Red Bird Airport. The instructor is all smiles, happy for me, reminding me how well I'm going to do. As I walk around the plane doing the final check, I feel at least a foot taller. In the cockpit, going down the preflight checklist before takeoff, no instructor beside me, I'm confident. The takeoff is perfect, effortless. Flying at cruising altitude, I look down at the greens and golds of the treetops, the rich black of the plowed Texas fields. I'm here. I'm alone. I notice the endless horizon...

I can do anything. Go anywhere.

Notes on Crow

As the crow flies - straight
                              direct

NO dilly dally - ALIVE

   Looking Marking Making

NO nonsense
NO absence
NO make sense

   AWAKE   Seeing   Being

On the brink
On the edge   ledge

Dredge it out of

NO where

   you can see

          be

             feel it!

en·thu·si·asm

n. [Gr. *enthousiasm*
to be inspired
by a god, inspir

The Gamble

The ancient elevator balked before starting its descent, taking me to my job with a travel agency in the basement of Titche's Department Store, the job I'd gotten after Denny's. I thought to myself, "I can't do this one more day."

All day I helped people plan cruises to the Mediterranean, describing the sumptuous meals they would enjoy on board ship, while the smell of over-cooked broccoli and pot roast wafted over from the basement cafeteria. Even fresh roses from my aunt's garden couldn't brighten up the cave-like atmosphere.

At lunchtime, threading my way through bargain shoppers elbowing each other between racks of mark downs, I escaped outside to the bright sunny September day. Walking a few blocks, I noticed the downtown campus of Dallas College and went in, just to see what was available. Day classes in drawing and pottery were open. I signed up, went back to the office, and quit my job.

It was a gamble, a long shot, but I knew I was at a big crossroad. I was thirty three years old, just out of a third divorce, living with my Aunt Nina. Most of my family and friends wondered whether quitting a good job to go to art school was such a great idea. My only means of income would be a part time job waiting tables.

Aunt Nina was my lone family supporter. She said, "Why, Janice, that's great. When you were a little girl, you loved to play in the mud!" My friend Pat cheered me on. I hoped I hadn't gone off the deep end.

chance

1. fortuity;
   luck
3. a risk

6. a possibility

Going to art school was even more exciting than I expected. Paint, clay, bronze, art history became my world. Learning to use a potter's wheel, feeling the clay, seeing the piece take form in my hands, I knew what I wanted to do for a living. The following term I registered full time, getting loans and scholarships.

After two years I graduated and moved back to California. I found a job teaching classes at a pottery studio. The day I quit my job at the travel agency was the day I started my real life. Herb Caen was right.

John

Another minute and we would have never met. He was just turning to leave when I came out of the bathroom of the pottery studio where I worked.

"Hi," I said, "Are you interested in pottery classes?"

"Yes, but the man in front said they're full."

"There's one starting Tuesday evening with space for one more."

As I was describing the class, his young son came in. "Dad, when are you coming? We need to go."

He saw my expression fall. We had been carrying on a conversation with our eyes while we were talking about pottery class schedules. He quickly said, "Oh, my weekend children are with me. I'd better go, but I'll be back Tuesday."

John was already there when I arrived that night, a little late from my day job. Working together, wedging clay, I asked him about himself. Divorced, three children, he liked to make art. I wasted no time telling him about me. I'd just graduated from art school in Texas at age thirty five, then moved to California and found the job at the pottery school. I also told him about the three divorces. If the relationship was going to go anywhere, I wanted it to be authentic; no sugar coating the past. He later said what he thought about the divorces... "By now, she must really know what she wants."

When class was over, I asked John if he would like to go for coffee. Between bites of tuna sandwich, he said he had majored in art, married during college, and when children started coming, made a living first painting houses, then as a Sears mechanic. He continued making art, but had no time to develop a career as an artist. From odd scrap parts he had built a potter's wheel in his garage. That impressed me.

The next class I asked him over to my apartment. We drank Ovaltine and talked about art. After the third class, with no invitation coming from him, I was about to leave alone. It was time for him to make the next move. Just as I was going out the door, he caught my eye. Motioning with his fingers held to his lips like he was holding a cup, he smiled. Thank goodness! I hadn't just imagined his interest after all.

mine[1]

that or those
belonging to me
the absolute form of *my*

That night, as I pictured a white cottage in the country I heard myself saying, "John, would you like to have a pottery studio together?" Another voice in my head said, "What did you say? You barely know this man." John looked surprised. "No." he said. "This is just a hobby."

A few weeks later, on Thanksgiving Day, I was counting my blessings, savoring being in California, finding the job at the pottery. I went for a long bike ride through the golden hills of San Rafael. Later I called John and invited him to dinner the following evening. He said it was his weekend with the children, but could I have breakfast with him on Saturday morning and meet his children.

Early Saturday morning, we had waffles at the Pink Poodle Diner. (I think he was checking me out to see if I enjoyed good food at a down home place, or did I need a more fancy atmosphere.) Then we picked up his children, Jonah 10, Jesse 8, Sara 5, all blue-eyed blondes, just like he was...and they did their own appraisal of me. John took me to work at the pottery, and in the afternoon, we took the kids for lunch. Getting to know each other was easy, comfortable, and exciting.

We saw each other often, went to art galleries, museums, art festivals. Every night we met at the pottery, and after a few months rented our own studio. That winter, John asked me to share his "bungalow by the bay," a 7 x 11 foot travel trailer he lived in since his divorce. In such a small space we worked out differences fast. There was no going into another room when we had disagreements. It had to be talked about knee to knee in the tiny space. We celebrated Christmas of 1974 there in a tangle of gifts and wrapping paper with his three children and my four year old nephew Anthony, who loved his new cousins.

The next year, we bought three acres in Sonoma Valley, complete with a white cottage like the one I had fantasized having, and another cottage for the pottery. John built a kiln. We put a sign out by the road and opened our pottery with a gallery in the front room. Tourists stopped in and bought our work. What had seemed like an impossible dream to both of us became a reality.

trust
IE. base see TRUE
1. *a*) firm belief

2. confident
   expectation

Afterword

Unlike in fairy tales, real life stories continue after dreams come true, and we experience unexpected turns in the road. We closed the pottery after sixteen years to pursue other interests. My focus is painting and writing, and John's is sculpture, painting and digital art. We collaborate on projects when our interests converge. This book is an example.

We have discovered tools along the way which enable us to grow as individuals and in our relationship, and to be honest, we still feel like we're on our honeymoon, but even better. Feeding our creativity and nurturing a relationship is like tending a garden. New plants to add, weeds to pull, thinning and fertilizer are needed. It's all worth it.

Time

An hour is long enough
if you take it
but if you don't
it's way too short
and your life flies by
without you knowing
and you may forget
to go to Paris
and never know you missed it
since how would you get there
if you never stopped long enough
to imagine yourself?

be·ing   1. state of
existence or life

2. fundamen____ essential
____ompleteness

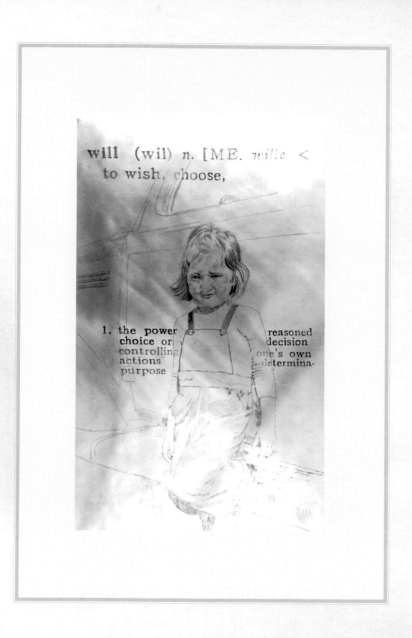

WHO'S GONNA GET THIS CLEENT UP ONCE AND FOR ALL?

You can play after you get your chores done
    1 dishes washt
    2 clothes arned
    3 weeds pult
    4 bills paid
    5 lists maid

In the meantime (Greenwich)

A lot of paintings went through her hands in the sink of dishes
A lot of poems got lost in the stack of bills
A lot of places to go, people to see
    never got visited
    while the weeds kept on coming
    and the clothes got dirty again again again

One day she walked out the door
And didn't take no clothes
And didn't take no dishes
And didn't take Bill, neither

All she had was a list in her mind of
    poems to write
    paintings to make
    walks to take in summer weeds
    people to see and places to go.

king (kin)

son of noble kin

monarch a man
highly cessful
supreme class
crowned supreme

can move
forward
direction any

Acknowledgements

Sitting side by side with John in our "pea green boat"* making the book together was an incredible experience. His creative eye and design talent provided the background for my paintings and stories.

Many people have been supportive to me, beginning with Don Gerrard, who first said this series of drawings and watercolors should be a book. From his initial enthusiasm, seconded by Don's wife and my dear friend Eugenia Gerrard, the project developed. I am deeply grateful to them for their unstinting love and encouragement.

I was fortunate to have extraordinary teachers. Bob Kinmont, my first watercolor teacher, provided the foundation to build on. Wayne Thiebaud and Jessel Miller gave me further invaluable guidance in painting. My dear friend June Hudson not only encouraged my first attempts at writing, she is also an important teacher and editor. Adair Lara's classes helped me immensely in developing the stories. Joseph and Cynthia Battershall were influential guides in my development of the child spirit.

Lilla Weinberger, Hal Zina Bennett, Mary Thompson, Carolynne Gamble, Alice Acheson, Jim Scott, Liz Curry, Stephanie Curry, Ann Nix and Deborah Hill made valuable editing suggestions.

My heartfelt gratitude goes to my family: J. J. Crow, Anthony Lupo, Erika Nelson, Fred and Hela Crown Tamir, Ed, Rose and Sarah Crow, Sheila and Jerrod Martin, Sally Crow, Joyce Hunter Gibson, Marlene Adams Phillips, Sara Blue Curry, Patrick Lazzari, Savanna Lazzari, Spencer Curry, Jon, Christine and Emma Curry, Charles and Maureen Curry, Barbara Curry, Meta Dillashaw, Elizabeth Grivas, Dorothy Kline, John Kline, LaJuana Sexton and many others all around the country whose love I appreciate.

Cherished friends have been an ongoing cheering section. They include Selma and Howard Aslin, Alex and Jan Kadrie, Pat Dickerson, Kaetie Bailie, Judith and Bill Moyers, John and Jean Painter, Heidi Porch, Dunstan Morrissey, Harihar Ram, Josh Kloepping, Jane Zimmerman, Marlie Wesner, Lindsay Whiting, Judy Theo, Natalie Sonntag FitzGerald, Peter Sonntag, Frances Freewater, Lee Doan, Amy Belser, Debbie Belser, Ernie Lacey, Tim Arnold, Joan Reibli, Jack and Lois Chambers, Arlene and Bob Stamp, Bob Blosser, Richard and Disty Thompson, Barbara Jacobsen, Patt Bettinelli, Robbie and Janine Cohen, Jenny Lopez, Adrian and Mary Martinez, and Rosie and Don Paluch.

*Pea green boat comes from a dream I had. I was telling people in a writing group that if they are having a problem starting to write, a good way to get going is to start a sentence with "Me and my honey with not much money went sailing down the river in a pea green boat...."

For information about workshops, retreats, and to order this book, write to us at starwae@vom.com. Visit the web site at Starwae.com.